PHILIP SHERIDAN

Crossing the River Lethe

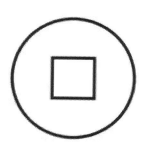

To Simon

Very warmest regards

Phil Shee

23/09/20

For my dad

'Power is in your heart beat.'
J.T.

Time is the substance I am made of. Time is a river which sweeps me along,
but I am the river;
it is a tiger which destroys me,
but I am the tiger;
it is a fire which consumes me,
but I am the fire.

JORGE LUIS BORGES

Contents

Acknowledgement

Thank you Alison Merrick, Denise Innes, Janet Cummings and Michelle Austin for your generous feedback and suggestions.

Thank you dad, you helped me so much with my reading and writing when I had so many difficulties at school. Finally diagnosed at the age of 42 having dyslexia.

Thank you Helen xxx

A Toast

To the broken and the worn out,
To the patina of a life lived well,
With all its wear and tear.

To the scars bared
On the skin and in the heart.

I'll raise a glass to you.

Blood

Blood is life.
I know this because the life saving gift of blood saved my life.

Blood is life.
I know this because blood speaks to us in our everyday
expressions:
Can't get blood out of a stone,
Blood is thicker than water,
Bloodshed,
In cold blood,
Makes my blood run cold,
Hot-blooded,
Bloods up,
Makes my blood boil,
Blue blood,
Fresh blood,
New blood,
Half-blood,
Runs in the blood,
Flesh and blood,
Young blood,
Blood-brother,

Blood-lust,
Bloodthirsty,
Blood-letting,
Bloody hell.

Blood is life.
I know this because when we speak of blood we feel a sense of carrying, containment and relationship, of kinship and love. Blood conveys our emotions, expresses our sense of self, enlivens the very essence of our nature.

Blood is life.
I know this because blood consists of 55% liquid plasma and 45% blood cells carried around the body within the cardiovascular system.

At the centre, our heart.
Blood flow pulses with our heart's beat.
One the action for the other.

Blood is life.
I know this because blood holds within its flow the life giving gases of oxygen and carbon dioxide that we exchange with our Earth's biosphere.
Blood affirms our relationship with all things.

Blood is life.
I know this because the protection of the circulation of blood remains the priority of doctors and paramedics around the world.

To save a life means the same today as it did before the advent of human blood transfusions in the 19th century – to stem the flow of blood when a vessel is cut or ruptured.

Blood is life.
I know this because to replace the lost blood as a result of trauma saves lives. Surgeons, no matter how skilled need blood transfusions to operate.

Blood is life.
I know this because someone, somewhere saved my life.
They gifted me their blood.

Without that gift, I would not live, nor love, nor breathe, nor have this rebirth,

This precious life I live.

Voices of a Patient

I speak
With a patient voice,
With a voice of care.

That knows the worth
Of a good life,
Abides in warm hearts,
That offer hot brews
With warm smiles.

That lives with the struggle,
Shared with those who know
Without confession.

That knows the worth
Of a good life,
Can't buy the hand that holds,
Nor the time that gives,
While pain has its gnaw.

That opens keen minds
To hear those things

One can only witness.

That knows the worth
Of a good life,
Unveils to young hearts
The human face,
Puts flesh on the bones.

Reveals a being,
Not a condition.[1]

The Return

I did not will myself back to life.

Other souls carried me
From the Styx and Archeron.

I bid Charon farewell,
My coin held safe for now.

Place

The world goes on you know,
With or without you.
History, that stuff that came before you,
Will happen anyway.

You do matter, don't ever forget it,
Why else would life make space for you?
No more or less but nevertheless,
You have your place.

The earth in her orbit,
Spins our nights into days,
Turns seasons into years.

While we weave cloth of word and deed
Into clothes of memory.

The flowers never stop blossoming,
The leaves never stop falling.
The earth keeps re-turning,
Never-ending,
Into being.

Life, that animus you call you,
Goes on you know.

Hózhó

Beside the River Worth,
I watched grey heron
Pluck brown trout.

Beak pierced,
Side speared,
Tail flapped.

Fish death,
Heron life.[2]

Sleep

I'm not going to sleep
In heavy limbed slumber,
I'm going to dream.

To live a plurality of lives
Beyond imagination.

Awaken amazed.

The Conference

I spied a siege of herons,
Gathered in a marsh
Of cotton grass and bulrush.

Their conversation kept secret
From my seat on the train.

Murmurings

A murmuration of starlings
Wheeled and turned
Above Doncaster.

A rare spectacular display
Seldom seen nowadays.

My heart held it's breath.

Depends

Who's story is it anyway,
Mine or yours?
If I'm the teller then I own it, don't I?
It's mine to say how it goes and why?

Depends.

The listener on hearing
may take it for themselves,
Change it in their mind to suit themselves.

Read between the lines,
Colour in and rub out where you did not,
Or dared not.

Make the story something more,
Or less than you first thought.

Now, it's not yours, or even theirs!
Because now someone else has heard it
And twisted it some more to their liking.

That's what happens when
You open your mouth.

The Wild and the Tamed

Peregrine flew down East Parade,
Peeled down Infirmary Street
In a silent glide toward City Square.

We the tamed
Walk beneath wild wings,
Pale imitations of a thing.[3]

One Dark One Light

One dark
One light.

Each must live with the other.
Think, speak, act with both voices present.

Decide which, upon which takes or gives,
Offers or withdraws.

One light
One dark.

Time and again you will fall,
Keep falling, falling forever.
Until you rise again, rise some more.

Test the waters with a toe nail tip,
Then a toe, followed by a foot.
With a feat of confidence submerge your knees.

Until you rise complete from the ground.
Swim with artful strokes,

Under a blue bow sky.

Under stars shining,
Carried in the milky river's flow.

Sin absolving, pollution dissolving in…

One dark
One light.

The Space Between

See this.

This space between us,
This gap that cleaves us.

Parts and gathers,
Flotsam and jetsam,
A rise and a fall,
Again and again.

See the delicacy
With which we approach one another.
You from there, me from here.

Appearances deceiving,
Disappearances regretting,
Things said, or not said.

Hopes and fears,
Glimpsed.

I think I see it

A flash of light, yes!
A school of thoughts turning.

Yes, I see it now.

The space between us.[4]

Crossing the River Lethe

You cannot take the river with you, she said.
You cannot know its train of thought.

Like these thoughts and memories,
That rise and fall in its turbid flow.

Lucid for a moment,
You reach out to hold on,
but they disappear.

You see,
I have changed and you have changed my dear.

They say that one can never step into the same river twice.
Well, I say that one can never step into the same memory either.

You see,
Everything flows my dear.

Water you cannot grasp,
Nor the wind can you comprehend.
Both come and go as they please.

Time passes.
Do you watch it go?
Or look for its arrival?

You choose my dear.[5]

The Song of Mind

The tongue sings,
The song of mind,
To the hearts beat,
While hands speak
Of stories told,
Round the fireplace,
Under moon and stars,
In the light of dark.

Thought Cast

Pitch a stone,
Cast a stone,
Throw another.

See the splash,
Hear the splosh.

Watch the ripples open outward,
Return inward.

Movement of movement
Of wave after wave,
Of peak after trough.

Of a stone picked
And flung from the ground.

Thoughts cast,
Thoughts thrown,
We pitch toward an unknown ending.

From which ripples spring,

That perhaps never end,
Until we stop throwing stones.

2017

And slowly at first,
But with the inevitability
Of the incoming tide,
Or the setting sun,
e world we once knew
Began to unravel.

Words Worth

What if words worth
Comes not from within but from without?

What if words
Come not from in-dwelling acquisition,
But ride upon forms outside?

That call to our foundling ears.
Inspire on entering
The embodied spiritus sanctus.

Bless us with pebbled thoughts,
Before we drop them in the babbling flow.

Drench the air
With streaming speech,
With a meaningful wind.

Sea Glass

I like sea glass
and fallen walls.

Cracked plates
and broken plaster.

A hole in a roof
Where the sky leaks in.

I like dripping taps
and half sunken boats.

Worn jean knees
and sweater elbows.

Chipped cups
and torn paper.

I like driftwood
and worn tires.

Leftover bread

and a crooked lane.

A threadbare shirt
with scarred skin underneath.

The Virtue of Shade

The tyranny of light,
The bright gaze of day.
All animals know the virtue of shade,
Avoid the glare of the bright.

Know the business of dreams lie at the heart of life.

Spartacus in the Library

Spartacus lives in my local library.
He rubs shoulders with Archer, Amis, Cartland, and Camus.
With Fitzgerald, Ginsberg, Heaney and Hughes.

He roams and sits with writers
Unbounded in the language of their tongues.
Who scribed thoughts to paper, any paper, anywhere.

Spartacus lives still.
One voice in a din of words and ideas,
That you, or I, can take from a shelf and read for free.

Spartacus, long dead, now lives in my local library.
Though they crucified him for speaking the truth,
He won in the end.

Litter Picking

Excuse me,
Excuse me!

She didn't stop.

I pick up the words she left behind.
Turn them in my hands.
Put them in my pocket one by one.

Pick them out one by one again.
When I get home
write them in my book.

Think about them from time to time,
Words left behind by someone else.
That fell upon my ears
At just the right time and place.

That I thought about giving back,
but for now, I'll keep them.
Place them with words of my own.

Give them some company, perhaps?

Set them in an order
Contrary to the intent of their speaker.

The work of a wordsmith involves
Just this kind of mundane litter picking.

Bread

Bread
Life.

Love
Life.

Don't need too much,
Just enough will do.

Bread,
Just say it.

Millenia wrapped in a word.

Earth trod by foot and hoof,
Seed sown by hand.

Smith craft for the reaping.
Clay for the baking.

Bread for the eating.

Roots

And the pine said,
Look, the roots of life lie all around you.
In your eyes,
And in the pungency of your nose,
And in the sweet-sour taste of your mouth,
And in the rough and smooth between your fingers and toes.

Longing for bare skinned feet.

Drunk Deer in the Night

"You're all confused!" Jonny said.

"We're all homeless now!
All travelers, traveling.

Our feet don't even touch the ground.
We step where we can,
Rest when rest allows.

We live in a land of no land,
Take our belongings with us,
The only belongings we have,
Our memories and our dreams.

We once walked in ancestor shoes,
Through groves of tall trees.
Once, we rode bareback ponies across waist high meadows.
Once, we picked cockles, and limpets, and mussels,
From seaweed strewn rocky shores,
And netted estuaries from coracles,
And feasted on the sea.

Now we walk on hard ground of our own making.
Bounded yet placeless among slabs concrete and stone.

A reservation life mistaken for a life lived on the land.

Land, once familiar,
Made a wilderness of someone else's making and keeping.

This earth,
This clay,
This embodied daemon,
Once lived and breathed before time and fences.

Only you can breathe life into your soul anew."

Jonny turned away,
Pressed shirt buttoned to the collar,
Blue Levi's immaculately ironed,
White Gazelle's gleaming in the fire light.

Campfire blazing light upon his face.
He turns, then disappears,
A flash of lightning in his hand,

A drunk deer in the night.

Syncopate

If you listen too hard
You just might miss the feeling

The hidden syncopated rhythm
That keeps our hearts

Beating.

Notes

VOICES OF A PATIENT

1   I began work on Voices of a Patient in November 2014. I felt inspired to write the poem from the conversations I had with and heard from my peers in the Patient Carer Community (PCC) based at Leeds Institute of Medical Education (LIME), University of Leeds.

In 2015 I produced a short film with members of the PCC and the late departed Dr. Kate Granger MBE. I dedicate this poem to the PCC members, to Kate, and all those who work in healthcare who take time to see the human being first, not a condition.

Voices of a Patient - https://vimeo.com/135677241

HÓZHÓ

2   In the Navajo worldview, *hózhó* describes life as a constant cycle of emergence and disappearance that we might roughly translate as *beauty*.

The River Worth flows down from Haworth Moor to the confluence with the River Aire in the small northern town of Keighley.

THE WILD AND THE TAMED

3   One cold and misty Monday morning in November as I walked up to the School of Medicine, at the University of Leeds, I saw an urban Peregrine Falcon.

THE SPACE BETWEEN

4   In October 2015 Bright Sparks Theatre Arts Company in collaboration with the Patient Carer Community (PCC) at the School of Medicine, University of Leeds, commissioned me to facilitate a series of poetry workshops for medical students exploring the lived experience of people and carers living with dementia.

In discussion with the students, carers and people living with dementia I

39

wrote the following poems, The Space Between, and Crossing the River Lethe.

You can watch two short films produced to reflect these wonderful workshops and the poems inspired by them with following links:

The Space Between - https://vimeo.com/171894508
Crossing the River Lethe - https://vimeo.com/171949045

CROSSING THE RIVER LETHE

5   One of five rivers that surround the underworld of Greek mythology, the River Lethe (pronounced Lee-thee) induces forgetfulness.

About the Author

Philip (b.1963) grew up in Yorkshire where he lives today.

In 2002 Philip survived a near fatal road traffic accident. He sustained multiple injuries including the eventual amputation of his right leg.

He published his first collection of poetry - Heart on the Mountain - in 2012.
Philip is a proud member of the Patient Carer Community at the School of Medicine, University of Leeds.

He works as a facilitator and mentor including Death Cafes.

You can connect with me on:

- https://www.philip-sheridan.com
- https://twitter.com/philsheridan888

Also by Philip Sheridan

Poetry that embraces life and death in equal measure.

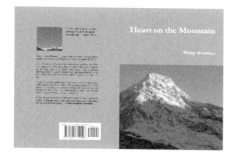

Heart on the Mountain

"Truly inspiring, moving, perceptive and thought provoking."

Printed in Poland
by Amazon Fulfillment
Poland Sp. z o.o., Wrocław

62213736R00033